THE MEMORIAL SECTION of the YIZKOR-BOOK of RAKISHOK and ENVIRONS

This book is the English translation
of the Memorial (in Rememberance) Section
(Pages 539 to 620) of the Yizkor-Book
of Rakishok and Environs.
The book was originally published in Yiddish
in 1952 by the Rakishker Landmanschaft
of Johannesburg, South Africa.
The Memorial (in Rememberance) Section has been
translated into English by Bella Golubchik.

The full proceeds from the sale of this book goes to
Arcadia Jewish Children's Home in Johannesburg and
any royalties from online sales of this book goes to the JDC,
The American Jewish Joint Distribution Committee

Compiled by David Solly Sandler

National Library of Australia Cataloguing-in-Publication entry

Title:	The Memorial Section of the Yizkor-Book of Rakishok and Environs Bella Golubchik has translated this book from Yiddish into English David Solly Sandler has compiled this book
ISBN:	9780992468477 (paperback)
Notes	Includes index.
Subjects:	Yisker-bukh fun Rakishok un umgegnt Yizkor-Book of Rakishok and Environs Memorial books (Holocaust)--Lithuania--Rokiškis Holocaust, Jewish (1939-1945)--Lithuania--Rokiškis World War, 1939-1945--Atrocities--Lithuania--Rokiškis. Jews--Lithuania--Rokiškis
Other Creators/Contributors:	Golubchik, Bella, translator Sandler, David Solly, Compiler.
Dewey Number:	940.53185793

The front cover is the original 1952 front cover of the book designed by Herman Wald

Every effort has been made to incorporate correct translations, information, dates, statistics and photos. The publisher regrets any errors and omissions, and invites readers to contribute their up-to-date or additional relevant information to:
    David Solly Sander, E-mail: <sedsand@iinet.net.au>

All rights reserved. No part of this publication may be reproduced, stored in a retrieval system or transmitted in any form or by any means, electronic, mechanical, photocopying, recording or otherwise, for profit making purposes, without the prior written permission of the copyright holder.

Copyright © David Solly Sandler 2014

ISBN 978-0-9924684-7-7

The Memorial Section
of the Yizkor-Book of Rakishok and Environs
translated into English by Bella Golubchik

Foreword

Bella Golubchick, who has translated the *Memorial Section of the Yizkor-Book of Rakishok and Environs* into English, introduced me to the book and told me about her close family connection to it:

"Ethel (Schwartzberg) Aarons and Yerachmiel (Ralph) Aarons are my parents.

I watched the book being brought to life by the members of the Rakishker Landsmanscaft in the dining room of my parents *palace* in Mayfair Johannesburg. I think every family contributed an article and (or) photographs. The book was edited by a man whose surname was Bakalczuk-Felin (Wonder of wonders- the first Jew I had ever heard of with a double-barrelled name) and his wife. They were indeed interesting times.

The woodcut on the cover was done by a truly great Jewish artist. Herman Wald. He is the sculptor who did the Holocaust Memorial on the Jewish cemetery in West Park Johannesburg. If I remember rightly he was paid ten pounds for it. (I stand to be corrected). My mother gave a number of copies of the book to the Jewish Board of Deputies Library. I don't know if the library still exists as it was.

I have also found a lot of very interesting things on *Google* under my mother's name and my father's name."

Bella sent me the articles written by her parents and photos of her parents and grandparents.

In my humble opinion the articles, stories and memories in the book, more than any other book I have read, tells us about Jewish life in Lithuania as it approached its destruction and end and Jewish life in early South Africa.

At the time I was collecting Jewish family histories and memories for a compilation *Our Litvak and South African Jewish Inheritance* and wanted to publish the complete book in English. Jewish Gen, who had translated about 80% of the book into English already, told me that they intended to do this themselves and so Bella and I have helped them; Bella by doing translations and I with copying photos and formatting them with the text.

PG Jewish Gen will publish the complete *Yizkor-Book of Rakishok and Environs* book in English soon and PG my compilation *Our Litvak and South African Jewish Inheritance* will be completed in 2015.

This translation of the Memorial Section of the book with photos was sent to Jewish Gen some months ago to incorporate into the book they are publishing.

David Solly Sandler   November 2014

The next four pages are from the original Yizkor-Book of Rakishok and Environs book

YIZKOR-BOOK of RAKISHOK and ENVIRONS
1952 ORIGINAL INNER COVER

YIZKOR-BOOK of RAKISHOK and ENVIRONS 1952
ORIGINAL INNER COVER

YIZKOR-BOOK

OF

Rakishok and Environs

issued by

The Rakishker Landsmanschaft of
Johannesburg, South Africa

on the occasion of
the 40th year of its establishment
(1912-1952)

EDITOR:

M. BAKALCZUK-FELIN

Yizkor Book Publishing Council:

PRAESIDIUM:

R. Aarons-Arsch, A. Nach-Nochumovitz, S. Rubin.

MEMBERS:

M. Muskat, I. Michel-Michalewitz, S. Klass, M. Klavier.

Johannesburg, 1952-5713.

YIZKOR-BOOK of RAKISHOK and ENVIRONS

1952 ORIGINAL PREFACE BY MEILACH BAKALCZUK-FELIN

The Yizkor Book to the memory of Rakishsker Jewry and to the communities surrounding it has just been published, eleven years after the annihilation. The pattern of life in Rakishok was similar to that of many small-town Lithuanian Jewries. Here Jews lived as closely-knit, separate units, often discriminated against and not less often in fear. But though there were sufferings there were also tranquil years with their measure of joy. But through all vicissitudes the Jews of the Lithuanian villages held steadfastly to the tenets of the faith and to their spiritual and cultural heritage.

Typical of the Jews' capacity for adjustment, they learnt to adapt themselves to changing circumstances, keeping aflame the hope for better days. Then came Hitler's murderous hordes; and in 1941, in a matter merely of weeks, the Jewish inhabitants of most of the Lithuanian towns and villages were led away like cattle to the slaughter. It was harvest time, and the reaper of death harvested all of Jewish life – the aged, the women, the children – none were spared.

Eleven years have slipped away since the holocaust, but the wounds have not been healed, and while the enormity of the tragedy is difficult to comprehend, there are those in our midst, and many of them, for whom the annihilation was a very personal tragedy in addition to being a Jewish tragedy.

It was, in all probability, this personal factor that partly stimulated the members of the Rakishker Landsleit Society to bring out the Yizkor Book. After all, a book is still the most enduring memorial to a past that has perished. The sponsors of this book set themselves three main tasks when they undertook to issue this tribute to the memory of their brethren in the far-off villages from which they themselves, or their forebears once came. They wanted to reflect the pattern of Jewish life in those villages up to World War II; they wanted to save from oblivion the memory of the ghastly era of Destruction; and finally they wished to place on record the activities of the Rakishker Landsleit in South Africa, during the forty years of the existence of their Society.

To implement these aims required considerable thought and responsibility. Every Jewish community in the old world had its own specific pattern: it virtually possessed individuality, but to convey this was no easy matter, for the simple reason that there are today large gaps in the historical sources which precluded the possibility of rendering a picture of that life in its entirety. In addition, no real authentic documentation of the last days of Rakishok was possible because there are almost no survivors who could have filled out the record.

YIZKOR-BOOK OF RAKISHOK AND ENVIRONS

1952 ORIGINAL PREFACE BY MEILACH BAKALCZUK-FELIN

CONTINUED...............

A very few may have escaped and they may today be in the U.S.S.R., but it was quite impossible to establish contact with them. With regard to the third aim, it was extremely difficult to piece together the story of the activities of the last forty years here from the inadequate minutes in existence today. Despite these difficulties the sponsor thought that the work was worth while, and the Yizkor Book contains important material hitherto unpublished: reminiscences, descriptions of the economic conditions of the various villages and their social and cultural institutions. Humble and poor though most of these Jews were, the material that the Rakishok Society had to sift through disclosed men and women of superb ethical and moral qualities.

The Yizkor book also sheds new light on the forces at work between the two world wars which helped to shape and modernise Jewish national life in the Lithuanian villages. It discloses the social changes which were taking place and the rising consciousness towards our national renaissance, which these people were imbued. Although, as previously mentioned, the compilers were unable to obtain first-hand reports from actual survivors of Rakishok, they were, however, able to secure eyewitness accounts of the destruction, and the merciless cruelties of the Germans and also the Lithuanians. Through documents they were also enabled to trace some of the activities of the Rakishker landsmanschaft, disclosing as they do the wide range of social activities of the old country. These documents reveal, in no small measure, the spiritual and cultural heritage with which we owe to those who perished. In fact, the Yizkor Book, with its illustrations, is an important historical monograph, not only for the Landsleit. It is a contribution to the history of the destroyed Jewish communities of Eastern Europe.

Finally, the Yizkor Book is a human document: a tribute to the simple God-fearing Jews of the villages who lived their lives, simply and genuinely, with those peculiar folk-ways evolved by Jewish Lithuania.

Those who laboured so zealously to bring out this Yizkor Book will be fully compensated if the Yiddish public will find in its pages its intrinsic message, the message of a human and historic document.

INDEX OF THOSE REMEMBERED
in the MEMORIAL SECTION of the
YIZKOR-BOOK of RAKISHOK and ENVIRONS
Original (old) pages 539-620 - Now (new) pages 1-82
Translated into English by Bella Golubchik

	PAGE Old	New
Abramowitz Rasiah–Beileh, husband Abraham and children Hershel, Zelig, Yechiel	556	18
Aires Yitzchak, wife Pessia and children Taibeh, Yiskeh and Binyomin	605	67
Arsh Elchanan and wife Nachama-Liebe	561	23
Ashkenazi Chatziah-Leib, wife Soreh-Leah and children Chayim Yishajahu, Chaikeh, Hirshel and Bashkeh	584	46
Bacher Yitzchak and wife Chayeh Soreh Ita	555	17
Bakalczuk Aharon	591	53
Bakalczuk Devorah	583	45
Bakalczuk Necha (Tabachowitz) and children Yosseleh and Devoreleh	558	20
Bakalczuk Soreh and daughter Feigeh	583	45
Bakalczuk Tzvi-Hirsh, wife Chaya-Miriam and children: Malka, Simeh, Moshe-Aharon	591	53
Bakalczuk Yehuda-Leib, wife Chaya and children: Berel, Aharon, Feigeh Malka, Brocheh, Sheineh-Yentel and Rochaleh	591	53
Baradavka Eidel and child	593	55
Baradavka Ethel	593	55
Baradavka Etta	596	58
Baradavka Hirsh	596	58
Baradavka Itzik	593	53
Baradavka Zalman	593	53
Beder Chayim, wife Shifra and children	556	18
Beder Dovid-Moshe and wife Esther Rochel	556	18
Beder Karpel, wife Soreh and children Rivka, Ya'akov, Yechiel, Yehuda, Yitzchak and Dovid-Moshe	556	18
Beder Pinye-Ya'akov, wife Liebe and daughter Asna	556	18
Berelowitz Chatzkel	608	70
Berelowitz Dov-Behr and wife Chasia-Tzireh	608	70
Berzack Meyer and wife Yenteh-Beileh	569	31
Berzack Mordechai-Peretz, wife Chaya and children Gedaliah and Gittel	574	36

	PAGE	
	Old	New
Beynart Moshe, wife Chayah and son Yaakov-Zelig	612	74
Blacher Abba and wife Tcherneh-Liebe	567	29
Blacher Alter Shein	567	29
Blacher Ya'akov-Ben-Zion, wife and children	567	29
Brinkman Abraham, wife and children	544	6
Brinkman Aharon, wife Chana and children	544	6
Brinkman Binyomin, wife Mineh-Tzibel and ten children	544	6
Brinkman Peiah, husband Alter Reve and children	544	6
Brinkman Yudel and wife: Hindeh-Matleh	544	6
Brinkman Zalman, wife and children	544	6
Bunimovitz Soreh-Pessah (Ginsburg)	611	73
Chaitowitz Avrohom Dovid, wife Ettel and son Rabbi Eliezer and his children Mottel and Hindeh and their families.	618	80
Charmatz Shmuel and wife: Soreh-Mineh	580	42
Davidovitz Yitzchak and wife Chaya	603	65
Dektor Azriel-Yehuda and wife Toibeh	566	28
Dektor Lyubeh	566	28
Dubiansky Chana-Elke	570	32
Dubiansky Feigetshkel	570	32
Dubiansky Notel, wife Reyzel and son	570	32
Dubiansky Sholem and wife	570	32
Dubiansky Yosef and wife Chaya-Soreh	570	32
Eidelman Avraham Yitzchak, wife Simeh and daughter Chyeneh	582	44
Eizenshtein Rodel and Devorah	583	45
Farber Miriam (Gandelman), husband and children	564	26
Farber Moshe Ya'akov Ha Kohein	581	43
Farber Sheineh (Epshtein), husband Chayim-Yosef and daughter	564	26
Fishman Hershel, wife Riveleh (Bakaltshuk), and children Aharon-Yitzchak, Motteh and Zeldeleh	591	53
Fleishman Shlomo-Yehuda and wife Frumeh	619	81
Friedman Shlomo and wife Tzippeh	590	52
Fulman Chayim-Itzeh	571	33
Fulman Ida-Feigeh and daughter Rivkah	571	33
Fulman Mereh, husband Leibeh and children	571	33

	PAGE	
	Old	New
Galperin Rivka husband and children	573	35
Gamburg Bassel and husband Velveh and children	586	48
Gen Chayim-Moshe	619	81
Ginzburg Aharon and wife Leibeh-Blumah	589	51
Ginzberg Chana-Musiah	611	73
Ginzberg Chayim Dov-Behr and Moshe (Brothers)	589	51
Ginzburg Feigeh and husband	589	51
Ginzberg Yosel-Raphael and wife: Rivka	611	73
Ginzburg Yosef- Rafael, wife Rochel and children	589	51
Gofanowitz Chaya, husband Moshe Yitzchak and children Soreh, Reizeh, Taibeh, Frida and son Aryeh Leib	556	18
Gordon Goldeh, husband Nottel and children Yosef, Leib, Zeldeh and Itzik	584	46
Gordon Nottel	557	19
Gordon Nottel and wife Goldeh	584	46
Gordon Rikleh	584	46
Grif Yisroel-Moshe and wife Feigeh-Rochel	580	42
Gringut Chayim-Yitzchak, wife Matleh and sons Rafael and Chone	610	72
Gringut Esther (Shlosberg)	610	72
Gringut Refael	610	72
Griz Ella	588	50
Griz Mendel-Leib	588	50
Hesselowitz Moshe and wife Reizel	580	42
Hurwitz Avrohom Refael, wife Ita and children	545	7
Hurwitz Efraim Yitzchok, wife Bassel and children	545	7
Hurwitz Leibe, wife and child	545	7
Hurwitz Shlomo and wife Soreh-Leah	567	29
Hurwitz Uri-Leizer and wife Ettel	545	7
Ichilchik (Yichiltshik) Yitzchak, wife Sonia and children Mendel, Henieh-Rochel and Zeldeh	618	80
Ida (Riback), husband and children, son in law and grandchildren	577	39
Itzikman Yerachmiel and family	586	48
Itzikman Yisroel, wife Chiyeneh and daughter Chaya-Devorah,	586	48
Jacobson Beileh, husband Yankel and children	584	46
Jacobson Yechezkel, wife Soreh and son Immanuel	582	44

	PAGE	
	Old	New
Kalakur Musieh, children and grandchildren	604	66
Karabuz Elieh-Leizer, wife Soreh and son Moshe Zelig	579	41
Kark Ya akov, wife Guteh-Leah and children Dvorah, Yochkeh, Yehuidit, Leizer and Leib	607	69
Katz Berel, wife and children	614	76
Katz Chaya-Genendel	600	62
Katz Mottel and family	577	39
Katz Mottel, wife Musheh-Batya and son Yudel	614	76
Kiel Avrohom-Yudel	620	82
Klas Shaul Gershon	548	10
Klas Zviah	548	10
Klatzkin Avrohom and wife	573	35
Klatzkin Mendel, wife Chassel and daughter Rivka Galpern and husband and children	573	35
Klavier Zelig-Dovid, wife Tileh-Ida and son Ya'akov	573	35
Klein Yosef-Yitzchak, wife Mereh-Feigeh and son Menachem-Mendel	612	74
Klug Liebeh, husband Chayim and children	588	50
Klug Michoel and wife Tzippeh	588	50
Klug Nechemiah and Moshe	588	50
Koppelowitch Isser, wife Henieh (Yaffe) and son Nochemkeh	617	79
Koppelowitch Nachman, wife Liebeh and sons Leizer and Zalman	617	79
Kremer Chayim and wife Chayah-Soreh	619	81
Krengle Tziporrah (Ruch), husband Yitzchak and children Chana and Yisroel	585	47
Kriel Yitzchak Boruch and wife Chana-Riveh	584	46
Krook Avraham, wife and children	563	25
Krook David, wife and child	563	25
Krook Menachem-Mendel	563	25
Krook Rochel and children: Reineh, Soreh, Tzippeh, Gershon, Shlomo and Berel	563	25
Kuklavsky Shlomo, wife Chayeh-Itah and children	543	5
Kuperman Mendel	612	74
Kur Yankel-Hirsheh, wife Soreh and son Faiveh-Behr	601	63
Lande Esther-Goldeh (Bakaltshuk), and husband Abraham	591	53
Lapp Michoel	543	5

	PAGE	
	Old	New
Levin Aharon and wife: Merel (Dubiansky)	570	32
Levin Aryeh son of Yisroel and wife Soreh-Riveh	584	46
Levin Chatzkel	567	29
Levin Fishel and wife Sheineh-Rochel	597	59
Levin Mendel-Leib, wife: Soreh Frumeh and children Shmuel, Henyeh and Leivik	546	8
Levin Ya'akov, wife Feige and children Pereleh and Maneh Leizer	546	8
Levin Yona and wife Chaya-Leah	560	22
Lubowitz Avrohom-Mendel and wife Ettel	603	65
Lubowitz Shaul, wife Chaya-Dvorah (Wingrin) and four children	594	56
Michalewitz Michoel-Ze'ev and children Moshe and Frumkeleh	613	65
Mikel Nachama-Sheine and son Choneh	550	12
Miller Bentzieh, wife Soreh-Leah (Fulman) and daughter Chashkeh	571	33
Moskowitz Soreh	576	38
Moss Meier (Shmuskowitz)	609	71
Muskat Shmuel-Natan and wife Feiga	608	70
Nochumowitz Beinash and wife Rochel Gittel (Barris)	542	4
Nachumowitz Chayim-Yitzchak and family	604	66
Nachumowitz Menachem-Mendel	604	66
Nachumowitz Refael son of Aharon and wife Heniah-Malkah	565	27
Orelowitz Abraham-Aharon	547	9
Orelowitz Choneh, wife and children	578	40
Orelowitz Freida and husband Avraham and children	578	40
Orelowitz Mayer-Leizer, wife Dobra and son Ben-Zion	578	40
Orelowitz Pesach, wife and children	578	40
Orelowitz Rochel-Ita, husband and children	578	40
Orlin Avraham-Aryeh and wife: Rochel	568	30
Pakawitz Leizer, wife Soreh-Leah (Aires) and four children	605	67
Penkin Reizeh-Dobra (Ruch) and husband Katriel	593	55
Perkis David and wife	612	74
Perkis Reyzeh, Leah and Beileh (sisters)	612	74
Podlass Braineh, five married children and grandchildren	584	46
Podlass Michael	584	46
Podlass Yankel, wife, children and grandchildren	584	46

	PAGE	
	Old	New
Pogrund Chieneh and Reuven Meier (siblings)	615	77
Pogrund Feige-Blumah, husband and son	615	77
Pogrund Nochum-Nottel and wife Pessel	615	77
Pogrund Yitzchak, wifeHenieh and children Meier, Zalman and Tzileh	616	78
Radeh Tuvia, wife Chyeneh (Eidelman) and children Yitzchak, Chaya-Henyeh, Leib, Peretz, Chana and Ben-Zion	582	44
Reef Elieh Hirsheh and wife Zeldeh	592	54
Rosenberg Soreh-Neleh, husband Dovid and children	610	72
Rozenberg Henach, wife Mineh (Gringut) and children	610	72
Rubin Aharon-Natan and wife Irleh-Brochah	595	57
Rubin Shlomo, wife and children: Dovid-Lazar, Leibeh	596	58
Rubin Soreh-Rivka	596	58
Ruch Chaim-Yerahcmiel, wife Chaya-Batya and children Heinieh, Iteh, Keileh, Leibeh, Gitteh-Zeldeh, Hirsh and Leah	592	54
Ruch David and Yissacher (brothers)	585	47
Ruch Elchanan Zelig, wife Chaya-Zeldeh and daughter Chana	585	47
Ruch Avraham-Koppel and wife Liebeh (Wolf) and sons Michal-Yitzchak and Yudel	554	16
Ruch Meier and daughter Soreh	585	47
Ruch Pereh-Ida	585	47
Ruch Reuven and wife Rochel	572	34
Ruch Shmuel, wife Leah and daughter Michleh	585	47
Ruch Tzipporah, husband Yitzchak Krengel and children Chana and Yisroel	585	47
Ruch Yehoshuah Zelig, wife Esther and daughters Chaitzeh and Pereleh	585	47
Ruskind Family	608	70
Sabel Dovid and wife Sheineh	575	37
Sacks Abba and wife Chana	553	15
Saitowitz Avrohom-Ya'akov and wife Mineh and son Gershon	570	32
Saitowitz Rochel-Frumeh and Genendel (sisters)	570	32
Saitowitz Sh'merel and wife Soreh-Rasheh	570	32
Saitowitz Zundel wife and children	570	32
Saltuper Yerachmiel and wife Peseh Maliyeh	551	13
Schwartz Shlomo and wife Esther (Baradavka)	596	58
Schwartz Yosef, wife Batya-Ettel and son Yitzchak	614	76
Schwartzberg Ya'akov-Shimshon and wife Esther Braina	540	2

	PAGE	
	Old	New
Segal Eliyahu, wife Ereh (Ashkenazi) and five children	584	46
Segal Faivush and wife Tziviah	588	50
Segal Family	543	5
Seratzhik Yisroel, wife Sheineh-Dobra and daughters Malkah and Soreh-Leah with husband Moshe Skurkewitch and children	619	81
Shapiro Hertzl, wife Rochel-Gittel and family	577	39
Shapiro Hertzl, wife Rocheh-Gittel and children	552	14
Shapiro Noach-Zvi and wife Matleh	552	14
Shapiro Zalkeh and wife Soreh-Buneh	588	50
Shlosberg Arkeh.Shimkeh and Motkeh(brothers)	610	72
Shmuskowitz Moss Meier	609	71
Shmuskowitz Yaakov	606	68
Shneider Eliyahu, wife Soreh-Leah (Klein) and child Michoel	612	74
Shneider Rivka-Dvora, husband Berel and children	545	7
Shneider Shmerel, wife Soreh and children: Avrohom-Moshe, Dobbeh, Riveh and Mineh	587	49
Shneider Familyl	599	61
Shribnik Soreh-Dinah, husband and daughter Feige-Rivkah	604	66
Shulman Liebeh, husband Yisroel and two children	586	48
Shusterman David Yitzchak, wife Soreh Beile and daughters Chyeneh, Elkeh and Chanyeh	541	3
Skurkewitch Moshe, wife Sarah-Leah (Seiratzhik) and children	619	81
Smilg Rikle and family	575	37
Snegg Binyamin and wife Mina- Tzibel and ten children	544	6
Snegg Ya'akov	559	21
Snegg Yisroel-Leib and wife Freidel	544	6
Sohn Soreh-Ettel (Katz), husband and children	614	76
Sommer Katriel and wife Sheineh	575	37
Spivak David, wife: Malkah and son Moshe	543	5
Swartzberg Chaya-Ita	562	24
Swartzberg Chayim Shimshon and wife Riveh-Giteh	573	35
Tzadok Soreh, husband and children Pesach, Yankel and Lazar	577	39
Tzindel Beileh and children	575	37
Tzukernick Chatzkel, wife Chaya and daughter Reizel	578	40

	PAGE	
	Old	New
Visakolsky Abba Yehoshua, wife Latteh Gittel and sons Yisroel, Moshe and No'ach	602	64
Visakolsky No'ach and wife	602	64
Wagenheim Chana, husband Herman and four children	589	51
Wiener Malkah Zamelan	614	76
Wiener Yudel	614	76
Wiener Hirsheh-Yankel and wife Dobra	614	76
Wineberg Mineh	586	48
Wingrin Berel and wife Rozeh	618	80
Wingrin Hertzeh and wife Toibeh-Riveh	594	56
Wingrin Avrohom-Leib and wife Henieh	594	56
Wingrin Soreh	594	56
Wolk Naphtali wife Chasia (Wingrin) and son	594	56
Yosselowitz Mendel (Witz)	574	36
Yosselovitz Menachem-Mendel	598	60
Yosselovitz Leibe-Hirsch, wife Beileh-Raiche and children Mendel (Witz), Isaac and Soreh	542	4
Yosselovitz Abraham, wife and children	542	4
Yosselowitz Hirsheh and wife Toibeh	570	32
Zageh Moshe and wife Goldeh	580	42
Zageh Tzviah and children	580	42
Zageh Zelig and wife Rochel	592	54
Zak Yaakov and wife Rivka	618	80
Zakstein Hayim-Ya'akov	615	77
Zakstein Leibeh and wife Henieh	615	77
Zakstein Shnaier-Zalman	587	49
Zamelan Leibel and wife Malkah	614	76
Zelikman Tzviah, husband and two children	549	11
Zilber Leibe	549	11
Zilber Leizer and wife Rivka	549	11

In Remembrance
(In Memoriam)

The MEMORIAL SECTION of the YIZKOR-BOOK of RAKISHOK and ENVIRONS
Original (old) pages 539-620 - Now (new) pages 1-82

Translated by Bella Golubchik

(The original book was assembled on the
dining room table of Bella's parents
in Mayfair Johannesburg
Bella's father, Mr R Aarons-Arsch
was a member of the Praesidium of
The Rakishok Landmanschaft)

**In Remembrance
[In Memoriam]**

of our Parents

Ya'akov Shimshon and

Esther Braina Schwartzberg

who died in

Kestell OFS

Orange Free State – South Africa

and were buried in
the Jewish Cemetery in
Bethlehem, Orange Free State

[from]

Sossel Rochel Abrams, husband and children

Moshe Schwartzberg, wife and children

Sheva Malk

Leah Gordon and Son

Ella Allen, husband and children

Stirel Cohen and husband

Yentel Gamsu and husband

May these few lines serve as a Memorial

In memory of our parents

David Yitzchak and

Soreh Beile Shusterman

[Aleihem Hashalom – May they rest in peace]

And of our sisters

Chyeneh [Chasyia]

Elkeh

Chanyeh

And their families

Who were born in Antalept
And perished in the Great Jewish
Destruction [Holocaust]
through the Hitler murder [extermination]

[from]

Their sons and brothers:

Shlomo, Hershel and Mottel Sher
and their families

In honour of
and as an illuminated memory of:
our father: **Leibe-Hirsch Yosselowitz**
who died in Rakishok in 1924
Of our mother: **Beileh-Raiche** who died in Rakishok
Of our brother: **Abraham Yosselowitz**
Wife and children who perished in Rakishok
Of our brother: **Mendel Witz [Yosselowitz]** who died in Johannesburg
Of our brother: **Isaac Yosselowitz** who died in Rakishok in 1914
Of our sister **Soreh Yellin** who died in Johannesburg

We will remember you all forever

[from]
Sachneh Lovitsch [Yosselowitz] and
Daughters in Durban

Chaykel Yosselowitz, wife and children in Israel
Yechiel David Lovitsch [Yosselowitz] – Durban

Gershon Witz [Yosselowitz] wife and children – Durban

Kalman Witz [Yosselowitz] – Durban

....
In Eternal Memory
Of Our Father

Beinash Nochumowitz
Who died 18th Cheshvan 1918 – Petrograd

Of our Mother
Rochel Gittel Nochumowitz-Bris [Barris]
Who died 8th Kislev 1951
Giv'at Brenner – Israel

We will always remember you!

[from]
Sonia and Koppel Barkai [Baradavka]
and children
Giv'at Brenner – Israel

Aharon Naki and wife Chaya – Cape Town

Moshe and Shalom Naki – Nochumowitz – Cape Town

We perpetuate the memory of
our Father

Michoel Lapp

Who died in Johannesburg

14th September 1942

[from]

Daughter:
Feige Rudnick
and
her husband

For our parents, brother and
sister-in-law

David and Malkah Spivak
And brother and nephew **Moshe**

Who perished in Rakishok
'May this be a Memorial

[from]

Son:Leib and
wife Luyba Spivak
and children

Sister Soreh and
Leizer Klas
and children

**In Memory of our brothers and
sister and families and the
whole large family
who were massacred**

by the Hitler murderers in Kurpletz,
a village near Rakishok

[from]

Henyeh and Asher
Jacobson [Yakobowitz]

Kayleh Segal,
husband and children

The memory is unforgettable
of our sister

Chayeh-Itah

and her husband

Shlomo Kuklavsky
and children

Who perished in Rakishok

[from]

Leizer and Soreh Klas and children
Chasiyah Friedman and daughter

For our Father: **Yudel Brinkman**

For our Mother:
Hindeh-Matleh Brinkman
who perished in Yuzhint

For our brother:
Binyamin Brinkman, his wife
Mushe and children who perished in Kamaiy

For our sister **Peiah**,
husband and **Alter Reve** and
their children who perished in Yuzhint.

For our brother **Abraham Brinkman**,
wife and children
who perished in the Churban Rakishok –
The Destruction of Rakishok

For our brother **Zaleh [Zalman] Brinkman** and
his wife and children who perished in Yuzhint

For our brother: **Ortchik [Aharon]**, wife **Chana** and
their children who perished in Yuzhint

For our uncle: **Yisroel-Leib Snegg** and his wife **Freidel**
who perished in the Destruction of Rakishok

For our cousin **Binyomin** and his wife **Mineh-Tzibel** and
their ten children who perished in the Destruction of Rakishok

May these lines be an eternal Memorial

[from]

Yerachmiel and Mineh Brinkman and daughters in Israel

Sareh and Moshe Mandel and Sons in Israel

Nathan and Leah Brinkman and children in South Africa

Yehoshuah Brinkman, wife and sons in Israel

Miryam and Yosef Gefner and daughters in Israel

We will never forget and always hold the memory dear [precious]
Of
Our Father: **Uri Leizer Hurwitz**
Who died 23rd Kislev 1938
Of
Our Mother: **Ettel Hurwitz**
Of
Our brother: **Efraim Yitzchok**, wife **Bassel** and children
Of
Our sister: **Rivka-Dvora Shneider**
Husband B**erel** and children
Of
Our brother: **Avrohom Refael Hurwitz**
Wife **Ita** and children
Of
Our brother: **Leibe Hurwitz**,
Wife and child

They were all martyred together with our Mother in the Destruction of Rakishok in 1941

We will remember you forever

[from]
Yisrael Moshe and Batya Hurwitz and children

Chayim Elyeh and Rivka Leah Hurwitz and children and grandchild – South Africa

Berel Hurwitz – America

Uri Leizer and Ettel Hurwitz

Berel and Rivka -Dvorah Shneider and children

May this be an eternal memorial
[in everlasting remembrance] of our parents

Mendel Leib and Soreh Frumeh Levin

Of our sister: **Feige** and
husband **Ya'akov Levin**
and their little children:
Pereleh and Maneh Leizer

Of our sister: **Henyeh**
and brother: **Leivik**
who perished in Churban Rakishok
[Destruction of Rakishok]

And in memory of our brother **Shmuel** who fell
in the slaughter by the German murderers
whilst fighting in the ranks of the Red Army

We will always remember you

[from]

Ya'akov and Chana Levin and children'

Chayim Yitzchak and Leah Levin and children

Shaiorka [Shaikeh] Levin and family

Gisa Levin

May this memorial [hazkarah]

be an eternal light

in memory of the

husband and brother

Abraham-Aharon Orelowitz [z"l]
[may he rest in peace]
who died 23rd August 1950
in Johannesburg

[from]

His wife Roseh Orelowitz and
Sister Musel Lewis

South Africa

[from]

Sister: Rodah and husband
Mordechai Beril and children

Sister: Chana Orelowitz

Sister: Dr Michle Orelowitz
and Shlomo Leibel

Sister: Nesyeh and husband
Dov Reznik and children

Israel

We will always remember the tragic death of
our unforgettable Father

Shaul Gershon Klas

Who perished by the hands of the Nazi Beast. He found his rest
in the common [communal, shared] grave, among 2,500 martyrs
somewhere in the vicinity of Abell.

He was in America for a short while, but in order not to desecrate
the Holy Shabbat [not to become secular] he travelled back
'aheim' – home, in order to be able to live in a
traditional Jewish spirit [atmosphere].

Of our Mother Zviah [Zivyah]
Who died 21st Shevat 1935 in Abell

May these few words serve as a memorial

[from] David Moshe Klas, wife and daughter
Johannesburg

The Unforgettable Parents
Leizer and Rivka Zilber

The sister
Tzviah Zelikman, husband and
Two children who perished in
The Destruction of Dvinsk

Tzviah Zelikman and her husband

Leibe Zilber

The Brother

Leibe Zilber

who fell as an
Heroic fighter in the Red
Army in Stalingrad

May this be a memorial

[from]

Yehudit and Pineh [Pinyeh] Merkel
and children

We express our deep and great sorrow
Over the death of our Mother

Nechama-Sheine Mikel

Who died in the Ponevesze hospital.
Prior to her death she sighed the following words:
'Where are you my far flung [flown far away] Children?'
She was buried in the Jewish Cemetery
[by Judaic rites] in Ponevesze on
Shemini Atzeret 1927

Over the death of our brother

Choneh Mikel

Who died in the 1st World War in the
Ukraine in the year 1916

We will remember you forever!

[from] Yitzchak and Yisroel Mikel [Michalewitz] – Johannesburg
Schimon Yosef Mikel – Michalewitz Pretoria with their wives and children–

We, children and grandchildren, will remember you

Forever dear and precious parents
Yerachmiel and Peseh Maliyeh Saltuper

We will remember our father and Zaida, who lived, all the years in agony,
as an invalid without legs. The image of our mother will always
appear before us; even though she was also a sickly [weak] woman,
she looked after our father with great love and devotion,
and in the final minutes [moments] going to the
Nazi pyres [bonfires], to the slaughter, she never
abandoned him even for a moment and together they underwent
the gruesome fate of their cruel death.

May their bones rest in the communal graves [brothers' graves]
of Eszhereni– Novo Aleksandrovsk.

[from] Moshe Israel and Mina Sharp – Saltuper and
children – Johannesburg.
Henye Silver, husband and son – Vilna
Yehoshua Shal and Eli Sharp Saltuper and daughters in Nairobi – Kenya

Noach Zvi and Matleh Shapiro

In Eternal Remembrance
of my parents

Noach-Zvi Shapiro

Who died 4th Teivet 1935

Matleh Shapiro

Who died 7th Teivet 1915

And of my brother
Hertzl Shapiro and his
Wife **Rocheh-Gittel** and
their children

who perished
due to the Nazi Executioners
[hangmen] in the Rakishok
Holocaust

In honour of their memory

[from]

Son and Brother

Morris Shapiro
With his wife and children
Johannesburg, South Africa

**Herzl and Rocheh-Gittel Shapiro
and Children**

We will remember and never forget
Our Father

Abba the son of Ya'akov Sacks

Who died in Johannesburg on 29th April 1941
2nd Iyar Tashä

And our Mother

Chana daughter of Tzvi Sacks

Who died in Johannesburg 10th October 1938
The 2nd day of Sukkot Tartzät

Your memory is holy and precious to us

[from]

Soreh-Rochel and Yitzchak Reef and children

Yosheh Sacks and wife

Sheineh and Kalman Yudelowitz and children

Zalman [Solly] Sacks and children

Baruch [Benny] and Dolyeh Sacks

In illuminated memory of
our Father

Avraham-Koppel B'R Leib Ruch

Who died in Rakishok 1st Tishrei Tarsäh

Of our Mother

Liebeh Bat Ya'akov Wolf

Who died in January, 26th Shevat Tarpäv

For our Brother

Michal-Yitzchak 'Ruch

Who died in Johannesburg 27th Sivan 1942

For our brother, husband and father

Yudel Ruch

Who died in Cape Town 2nd day Adar Bet 1932

We will not forget you and you will live forever in our hearts!

[from]

Toiveh Shneider and children

Asnah and Abraham Furman and children

Vitell and Faivush Klein and children

Soreh Ruch [wife of Yudel Ruch] and
children Liebeh-Viteh and Chayim Leib

On the Tombstone:

Our dear father:

Reb Yitzchak Ben Shaul Halevi.

Died 1st Shevat Tarpāg

In memory of our Father

Yitzchak [Alter] Bacher
who died 1st Shevat Tarpäg

For our Mother
Chayeh Soreh Ita
Daughter of Reb Abraham Koppel
who died 29th Av Tashäg 28th August 1943

We will remember you forever

[from] Chayim Shual [Ze'ev] Bacher, wife and children
Koppel Bacher, wife and children
Frieda Aron, husband and children
Ella-Etel Scop, husband and children
Meier-Moshe Bacher, wife and children
- South Africa
Debra Charney and husband and children – Bulawayo, Rhodesia

May this be a holy sanctifying and unforgettable
remembrance for our extended family

Father: **Dovid Moshe Beder**
who died Yom Kippur night 1937
Mother: **Esther Rochel Beder,**
perished [murdered] by the Nazis in Rakishok

Dovid Moshe and Esther Rochel Beder

Sisters: **Chaya Gofanowitz,** husband **Moshe Yitzchak** and children, **Soreh, Reizeh, Taibeh, Frida** and son **Aryeh Leib**

Rasiah – Beileh Abramowitz and husband. **Abraham,** originally from Antalep – a son of the famous **Antalepter Maggid** [Preacher] and their children **Hershel, Zelig and Yechiel,** who perished
together with the Jewish population in Rakishok in 1941 by the
hand of the German murderers.

Brothers: **Pinye Ya'akov Beder,** wife **Liebe** and daughter **Asna.** Perished in Posvel

Chayim Beder, wife **Shifra** and children, perished in Kovno

Karpel Beder, wife **Soreh** and children **Rivka, Ya'akov, Yechiel, Yehuda, Yitzchak** and **Dovid-Moshe** perished in Rakishok

And in memory of all the relatives and friends who perished
cruelly by the hand of the Germans in Lithuania.
We will remember your forever

[from]Your children, brothers, sisters and friends
Rivka and Ya'akov Miller and children
Shlomo Beder and family
Binyomin Beder and family
Yitzchak Beder and family

Our Brother
The Martyr

Nottel Gordon

Nottel Gordon

Who perished in Dachau together with 10,000 more other Jews.

We erect hereby a memorial [headstone]

for his eternal memory.

[from]
His brothers:

Berel, Michal and Yeshayahu Gordon
and their families

With these lines we erect an eternal Memorial to
Necha – our dear one who passed away
at the age 49 on 18 Sivan "Tashyäg 1st June 1953.

Necha [Nechama] Bakalczuk – Tabachowitz

She devoted her best years and exceptional talents to teaching in the public primary schools in Poland, in the displaced persons camps after the holocaust, and in South Africa. She was a wonderful personality, noble and aristocratic in her strength of character, in the beauty of her pure and innocent soul and in her love of our nation and its culture.

You, dear Necha, were saved from the flames of the furnaces, from the inferno of the Nazis, but you enfolded into yourself the period of horrors, that were stuck in your flesh like burning needles; and the tempest of nightmares that you experienced always floated before your eyes – together with the terrible tragedy that your children– **Yosseleh and Devoreleh** – were destroyed in the death chambers of Auschwitz. All these horrors, of the extermination camps, the tortures, the threats of death and conflagration that were organised by the wild animals, the accursed Germans, impoverished and weakened your health.

Those who remain are in sorrow and deep mourning.

Your husband: Your friend and companion
Meilach Bakalczuk
Your brothers: Simon and Yosef Tabachowitz and families

Original was in Hebrew not Yiddish

On the fresh grave
of our
unforgettable father and brother

Ya'akov Snegg

Who died on the first day of Chol
Ha Mo Eid Pesach the 12th April 1952

May this be in
Eternal Remembrance

[from]

Wife: Ita Snegg

Son: Abraham Snegg

Daughter: Yenteh [Iris Josephine],
husband Peretz Blum and sons

Daughter: Leah and husband Zelig Blesovsky

Son: Mottel Snegg, wife Yehudit and daughter:
Beileh and Moshe Finger and their
Daughter Yehudit Chana Snegg

Brother: Mottel Leib and Chana Snegg
Children and grandchildren [America]

To the everlasting and hallowed memory

Of our parents

**Yonah
and
Chaya – Leah Levin**

Yonah and Chaya-Leah Levin

Your children, who will remember you forever.

[from]

Avraham, Esther-Mineh, Moshe

Nathan and Israel Levin and families

In memory of our dear parents

Father: **Elchanan Arsh**

The nationalist [patriotic] modern Jew,
who never abandoned the threshold of the Shul.
Aristocratic of Spirit and wholeheartedly enthusiastic

Mother: **Nechama-Liebe**

The quiet woman, overflowing with an
abundance of good manners [gentility]

Who were slaughtered by Hitler and his cohorts
among the martyrs of Rakishok – Lithuania

Beloved and pleasant in their lives and
in their death they were not separated.

[from]

Rochel, Meilach, Yerachmiel, Bluma,

Avraham and David Arsh

And their families

Original was in Hebrew not Yiddish

Chaya-Ita Swartzberg

We will remember you forever

daughter and sister

Chaya-Ita Swartzberg

You will live in our hearts forever,
Holy martyr

[from]

Your parents
Hessel and Chana-Leah Swartzberg

Your brother
Efraim Swartzberg, wife Soreh Yehudit
and children

Your sister: Ethel and brother-in-law
Yerachmiel Aarons–Arsh and children

Your sister:
Soreh Yehudit and brother-in-law Yosef Kark and family

It pains the heart and the wound will never be healed,
knowing how our whole family perished.
The memory is eternally unforgettable of:

Our Father **Menachem Mendel Krook**
Who died in Varestzineh in 1922, 17th Tamuz Tarpäb

Of our Mother: **Rochel Krook**

Of the sisters: **Reineh, Soreh and Tzippeh**

Of our brother: **Abraham**, his wife and children

Of our brothers: **Gershon, Shlomo and Berel**

Who all perished in the Rakishok holocaust [destruction]
And of our brother: **David,** wife and child
who perished in Kupishok
No-one was saved from this extended [large] family
Your memory is holy to us

[from] Sachneh and Leah Kruger and son
Menachem Mendel and Reuven

May this be a holy memorial for our sister and aunt

Miriam Farber [Gandelman]

with her husband and children
Who committed suicide in Rakishok, in order not
to be transported to the Nazi scaffolds – to the mass graves

For our sister and aunt

Sheineh Farber [Epshtein]

For her husband **Chayim Yosef**
and their daughters

Who perished by the hand of the Nazi murderers
in S'vadosh

[from]

Your brother:

Nochum-Leib Farber, wife and children

Your nieces and nephews:

Rochel, Meilach, Yerachmiel, Blumah,
Abraham and David Arsh
and their families

May this be a light and eternal memory

For our Father

Refael B'R Aharon Nachumowitz

Who died 10th September 1937 – 5th Tishrei Tartzäh
In Johannesburg

For our Mother

Heniah-Malkah

Who died 28th November 1944 – 13th Kislev Tashäh
in Johannesburg

May this be a memorial

[from]

Rivka, Naomi, Soreh-Liebeh and Aaron Nachumowitz

We will, forever, hold the memory precious and holy

Of our sincere and devoted [faithful] parents

Azriel-Yehuda and Toibeh Dektor

Who perished tragically in Rakishok

Of our dear sister **Lyubeh Dektor**

who passed away in Moscow in 1943

We with our families, will never forget you.

[from]
David Dektor
Shlomo Dektor
Meyer Dektor
Merah Dektor-Melamed
Ida Dektor-Kantan
Chaya Dektor-Gordon
and their families

A memorial for our Father:
Shlomo Hurwitz
Who died on 5th Iyar Tarpäh

And our Mother:
Soreh-Leah who perished in
The massacre in Abell

For our brother-in-law
Chatzkel Levin
Who fell in the slaughter by
The German cannibals, near Riga

We will never forget you

Binyomin Michal and
Chaya Hurwitz and children
Freidel and Henech-Dovid Katz
Rochel Yaffe and her children
[South Africa]
Peretz Ze'ev and Liebe Hurwitz
Chayim Elia Hurwitz [America]

Soreh-Leah Hurwitz

We hereby perpetuate [the memory] of our parents:

Abba and Tcherneh-Liebe Blacher

Who died in Ostrachan in the First World War

And the Martyrs: **Ya'akov Ben-Zion Blacher**
Who was the Shochet [Ritual slaughterer] in Visinti
and his wife, may she rest in peace [neé Behr] and children

And the uncle: **Alter Shein 'Alav Ha Shalom'**
[May he rest in peace]
The Rosh Yeshiva in Slabodka, who perished by hand of the Germans,
in a tunnel, trying to hide the children of the Slabodker Ghetto in
sacks, wanting to save them from the German murderers.

Your memory is holy

[from] Nochum and Rivka Blacher and sons

We will always remember

our dear parents, Zaida and Bobba

Avraham-Aryeh-Tzvi Orlin

Who died in Kovno 8th Sivan 1941

Mother and Bobba

Rochel Bat Shraga-Feivish Orlin

Who died in Vilkomir 20th Adar 1938

You will live in our hearts forever!

[from]

Moshe-Chayim and Taibie Orlin and children
Yitzchak and Alteh Orlin and children
Azriel and Ettel Orlin and children
Dovid-Lieb and Riveh Orlin and children
Liebe-Yente and Moshe Gelman and children   )

South Africa

Chayah and Ya'akov Kaufman and daughter

Canada

May this be a holy memorial
For our unforgettable parents

Meyer Berzack
Born in 1883 and died 17th Iyar 1949

Yenteh-Beileh
Born in 1889 and died 19th Adar 1948

Both were buried in Cape Town, South Africa

Meyer and Yenteh-Beileh Berzack

Your shining memory will never be forgotten
Our ties to you are still very strong
[The feelings of being connected to you are for us,
your children, still very strong]

Their charity and good deeds have embedded themselves in the
hearts of Johannesburg Jewry and in us.

[from]
Mordechai, Leibeh, Yehuda, Moshe and Heinech Berzack, wives
and children in Johannesburg and Cape Town

For our Father **Sh'merel Saitowitz**
who died in Rakishok on 22nd Adar Tarpät

And our mother **Soreh-Rasheh** who passed away in
Johannesburg 8th Shevat, 10th January 1946

May these lines serve as a memorial

[from]
Rochel-Tziviah and Yitzchak Zinman children and grandchildren
Genendel and Motteh Goott
Pinyeh and Pessiah-Gittel Saitowitz children and grandchildren
Dovid-Berel and Esther Saitowitz and children
Aharon and Soreh-Leah Saitowitz and children

....

May this be in memory of our parents

Avrohom-Ya'akov and Mineh Saitowitz
And brother: **Gershon** who was martyred[in sanctifying Hashem] in Rakishok
And brother: **Zundel Saitowitz,** wife and children who perished in Shavell
And sister: **Rochel-Frumeh** who died in Rakishok 14th Elul 1921
And sister: **Genendel** who died in Vilna

[from]
Yisroel-Moshe and Tzipporah Saitowitz and children [in Kiryat-Chayim, Israel]
Soreh-Leah and Aharon Saitowitz and children [in South Arica]
Menucha-Rivka and Velvel Saitowitz and children [in South Africa]

....

We will always cherish the memory of our parents
Yosef and Chaya-Soreh Dubiansky who died in Abell

And of our brother **Nottel** and his wife
Reizel Dubiansky and sons who perished in Eszhereni

Of our sisters: **Chana-Elkeh, Feigetshkeh and
Merel,** and her Husband **Aharon Levin**
Of our brother: **Sholem Dubiansky** and his wife
Of our uncle and aunt **Hirsheh and Toibeh Yosselowitz**
Who all perished in Abell

Your memory is holy

[from]
Esther and Dovid-Berel Saitowitz and children

May this Hazkorah be an Eternal Light

For our Father:

Chayim-Itzeh Fulman

Who died in S'vadoshtz on 21st March 1929

For our Mother: **Ida-Feigeh Fulman**

For our sister: **Mereh**, husband **Leibeh** and children

For our sister: **Rivkah Fulman**

Who all perished in S'vadoshtz

For our sister:
Soreh-Leah, husband **Bentzieh Miller** and
Daughter **Chashkeh** who perished in Rakishok

The memory of all of you is holy!

We will never forget you!

Hindeh and Avrohom Merkel and children

[from]

Dinah Merkel, Chaya and Chayim
Lipschitz and children [Cape Town]

Leibeh and Rochel-Leah Fulman and
children [Boston, America]

Avrohom-Gershon and Fenyah Fulman and
children [Boston, America]

Chana and Yisroel Fushner and
daughters [Boston, America]

Our unforgettable parents

Reuven and Rochel Ruch

We, the sons and daughters erect here
on this 'Yizkor' Page, a memorial

in honour of your holy memory

In sorrow, your children who remained behind

[from]

Tuviah Ruch and family – Johannesburg, South Africa

Ahuva Ruch and family – Israel

Leah Ruch and family – Johannesburg

Latteh Ruch and family – Cape Town

Elchanan Ruch and family – Canada

Reizel Ruch and family – Canada

Sorrel Ruch and family – Canada

Avrohom Ruch and family – Canada

Ittel Ruch and family – America

Yerachmiel Ruch and family – Riga, Soviet Union

Chayim Shimshon Swartzberg

Let this be a memorial and

an everlasting memory [remembrance]

For our Father and Zaida

Chayim Shimshon Swartzberg
Who died in Worcester, America
24th Teivet Tartzä
13th January 1931

For our Mother

**Riveh-Giteh Swartzberg
[Bat Reb Yisroel-Tzvi]**
Who died in Rakishok 26th Adar Tarsä

[from]
Hessel and Chana-Leah Swartzberg
children and grandchildren

....

We Moshe and Chaya-Soreh Klavier express our great
sorrow over the cruel death

Of our parents **Zelig-Dovid and Tileh-Ida Klavier**
Of our brother: **Ya'akov Klavier**

Who were murdered by the German gangsters [bandits] in Abell

May these lines be an eternal memorial light
For our Father: **Mendel Klatzkin** who died in Yanishok in 1939
For our Mother: **Chassel Klatzkin**
For our brother: **Avrohom Klatzkin** and wife
For our sister: **Rivka Galperin,** husband and children

who all perished in Yanishok

We will never forget all of you

Your names will be engraved in our hearts forever

[from]Moshe and Chaya-Soreh Klavier and children

Mordechai Peretz Berzack

May this be
In everlasting memory

Of our Father
Mordechai-Peretz Berzack
who perished in Bagoslavishok.

Of our Mother: **Chaya Berzack** who
Died in Bagoslavishok in 1929

Of our brother: **Gedaliah Berzack**
Who perished in Keidan

Of our sister: **Gittel**
Who perished in Bagoslavishok

[from]
Reizel and Yisroel Michel-Michalewitz
and children – Johannesburg

Yentel and Reuven Novick and children – Pretoria

May this be a memorial

For my husband and the father
Of our children

Mendel Witz [Yosselowitz]

We will always remember you, who
are unforgettable

[from]

Malkah Witz and her children
Berel Witz and wife
Liebeh and David Kaplan
Binyomin Witz and wife
Beileh and Leah Witz

A hallowed memorial for our mother

Rikle Smilg

Who died in Johannesburg 5th [Menachem] Av Tarsät, 31st July 1944

And for our sister, brother-in-law
Goldeh and Nottel Gordon and children
who perished in the Rakishok Holocaust
and for all our relatives
who perished in the Holocaust of Lithuania

[from]
Moshe and Leah Smiedt [Smilg] and children

....

May this be a memorial for my
Beloved parents

Dovid and Sheineh Sabel

Who Passed away in Vryheid, Natal.
Your memory is holy and precious to me!

[from]
Sarah Jacobson

....

For: **Katriel and Sheineh Sommer**

For **Beileh-Tzindel** and her children

who all perished by the hand of the
German murderers in Rakishok

May this be an everlasting memorial for them!

[from]
Avrohom-Yisroel and Rochel Tzeredines
Miller – Oudtshoorn, Cape

On the new [fresh] grave of
My devoted wife and mother of our children

Soreh Moskowitz

Who died suddenly
Shabbat 7th Teivet Tashyäv 5th January 1952

May these lines be a hallowed and an
everlasting memory!

We will never forget her and always
remember her!

[from]

Chayim-Refael Moskowitz and
sons Shmuel [Sam] and Zalman [Zummy]
Daugher: Tamara and son-in-law Avraham [Arnold]
Tannenbaum and Granddaughter Hayley

I am deeply shattered by the gruesome murder
of my cousins:

Mottel Katz and family

Hertzl Shapiro,

wife **Rochel-Gittel** and family

and of the tragic deaths of all my friends
who were brutally murdered by the Nazi-cannibals
in Rakishok

[from]

Rochel Herr [Shapiro]

In Memoriam
[remembrance]
Of my beloved sister

Ida

With her husband and children,
Son-in-law and grandchildren

I will never forget you

[from]

Mirch and Yudel Riback

Johannesburg

I will never forget and
always remember
my beloved sister:

Soreh Tzadok,

brother-in-law and three sons,

Pesach, Yankel and Lazar

[from]

Yudel and Mireh Riback

Hereby, we erect a memorial
For our parents

Meyer-Leizer and Dobra Orelowitz

For our sisters:

Freida, husband **Avraham** and their children
Rochel-Ita, husband and children

For our brothers:

Pesach and his wife and children
Choneh and his wife and children
and for our brother: **Ben Zion**

Your memory is holy to us!

[from]
Chayim Leib and Beileh Orelowitz and children

....

May this be a memorial

For our parents

Chatzkel and Chaya Tzukernick

For our sister:

Reizel

Who perished tragically by the hand of the Nazi murderers.

We will never forget your tragic death!

[from]

Beileh and Chayim Leib Orelowitz and children

Elieh Leizer and Soreh Karabuz

Moshe Zelig Karabuz

We: daughters and sons

Perpetuate with this Hazkarah

[the memory] of our parents

Elieh-Leizer

and

Soreh Karabuz

who died in Cape Town

And our brother

Moshe Zelig Karabuz

Who died [serving] in the
South African Army
in the year 1944

We: Yossel Chayim
Ozer Yitzchak
Bezalel
Liebeh Gordon
Mineh Medin
Slava Paul

Will always remember you!

In hallowed memory of our sister
Reizel and her husband **Moshe Hesselkowitz**
who perished in the graves together with all the Rakishok Jews.
We will never forget you!
[from] Rivka, Naomi, Soreh-Leikeh
and Aaron Nochumowitz and their families

We will never forget our parents

Moshe and Goldeh Zageh
and our Mother and mother-in-law
Tzviah Zageh and children

who perished in Rakishok

[from]
Reuven Zageh and family
– South Africa
Rochel Roszhner-Zageh
- Israel

May this be an everlasting
memory [memorial]

For my sister
Soreh-Mineh and her husband
Shmuel Charmatz

And for my sister
Feigeh-Rochel and her husband
Yisroel-Moshe Grif
Who perished in Rakishok

[from] Hindeh Koppelowitch
and family

In memory of
Our father
Brother
and grandfather

The important [an illustrious] man,
exalted [very learned] in his knowledge of Torah

Moshe Ya'akov B"R Nochum Leib Ha Kohein Farber

Who passed away [was gathered to his people]
in Yerushalayim
On 2nd Kislev Tashyäg

At a full age [a ripe old age] being
97 years old

We erect this memorial to him

[from]

Nochum Leib and Necha Farber, children and
grandson – Port Elizabeth

Fanya Rubinshtein and daughters – Leningrad

Zalman Michal and Matlah Cohen and family

Rochel, Meilech, Yerachmiel, Blumah
Abraham and David Arsh

and their families

Original was in Hebrew not Yiddish

As an illuminated memorial

Of our father: **Avraham Yitzchak Eidelman**
Who died 12th Adar 1920 in Abell
Of our mother: **Simeh Eidelman**
Of our sister: **Chyeneh** and brother-in-law
Tuvia Radeh and children, **Yitzchak, Chaya-Henyeh, Leib, Peretz, Chana and Ben-Zion**

Who perished in Abell together with our
whole extended family

[from] Aryeh and Rochel Eidelman and family
Rochel Hurwitz – San Francisco

....

May this be an unforgettable reminder of our brother

Yechezkel, his wife **Soreh** and son **Immanuel Jacobson**

Who perished in Ezhereni

[from] Sister and brother-in-law
Rochel and Aryeh Eidelman and Sons

Soreh and Devorah [Dora] Bakalczuk

Feigeh [Felinkeh] Bakalczuk

I will never forget even to the last minute of my life that August dawn in 1942, under the heil of the Hitler-Fascist Bullets, at the ghetto fences, that we parted finally [fatally] and after that you perished tragically in the slaughter of Vohlin, Ukraine

You my dearly loved

Devorah [Dora] Bat Shlomo Chayim and

Rodel Eizenshtein from Pinsk and my only daughter
Feigeh [Felinkeh] Bat Eli Melech

and **Devorah Bakalczuk.**

You are for me, deeply tattooed and engraved in my soul and spirit.

The memory is unforgettable and holy of my dear and quaint mother

Soreh Bat Meir

whose soul expired on the first day of Rosh Hashanah 1940 in Sernik [Palesia]
Until I go into eternity, I will Remember you in great holiness [I will remember you until I die]

[from]
Elimelech [Meilech] Bakalczuk

We perpetuate hereby

Our Mother
Sarah-Riveh Bat Ettel Levin

Our Father
Reb Aryeh B"R Yisroel Levin

Our Mother
Chana-Riveh Bat Tzireh Kriel

Our Father
Reb Yitzchak-Boruch B"R Zisheh Kriel

[from]
Chana and Bunem-Idel Kriel
and their children

....

May this be a memorial

For our Husband and father:

Michael Podlass

Who died in Johannesburg,
South Africa

For my sister **Braineh**
with her five married children
and her grandchildren

For my brother
Yankel, wife, children and grandchildren

Who all perished in Melitopol
[Ukraine] by hand of the
Hitler murderers
[from]
Leah Podlass and children

For my brother
Chatziah-Leib Ashkenazi
and his wife **Soreh-Leah** and their children
Chayim Yishayahu, Chaikeh, Hirshel and Bashkeh
Who perished in the destruction of
Rakishok [the Rakishker Holocaust]

For our sister **Mersh**
with her husband **Eliyahu Segal**
who perished in Utian

For their five children
who perished with their families in
The Kovno Ghetto

May this be an eternal remembrance

[from] Ittel and
Yerachmiel Genn and family

....

May this serve as a holy
memorial [rememberance]of

My mother **Rikleh**
Who died in Johannesburg
31st July 1941 5 days in Adar

My sister: **Goldeh Gordon** and her husband
Nottel and their children: **Yosef, Leib, Zeldeh and Itzik**

My sister-in-law: **Beileh Jacobson** and
brother-in-law **Yankel**
and their children

and of all our relatives, who perished in the
last Great Holocaust

[from] Taibie Gordon and children

In holy remembrance

Of wife and mother
Pereh-Ida Ruch
who died in remote [far away] Siberia 16th Sivan 1952

Of our son and brother
Elchanan Zelig Ruch
who died in Rakoshok 14th Adar 1931;
and his wife **Chaya-Zeldeh** and daughter **Chana**
who perished in the Rakishker Holocaust

Of our son and brother
Meier and daughter **Soreh Ruch**

Of our brothers
David and Yissacher Ruch
Who were the first martyrs in Kovno, shot
by the Nazi executioners [hangmen] 21st June 1941

Of our daughter and sister
Tzipporah, who perished in the destruction
of Alita, with her husband **Yitzchak Krengel**
And their children, Chana and Yisroel

For our brother and uncle **Shmuel Ruch**
and his wife **Leah** and their daughter **Michleh**,
who perished in 'Rakishok

For our father, brother and uncle,
the beloved Rosh Yeshiva: The Rabbi:
Reb Yehoshuah Zelig Ruch,
with his Wife **Esther**
and daughters: **Chaitzeh and Pereleh**
Perished in Vilna Holocaust

[from]
Pesach Ruch, Leibeh and Gitteh Ruch
Berel and Chaya-Laykeh Ruch
And children
Batya Ruch
Meier-Leib and Soreh Ruch and children

May this memorial page be a headstone

For our Father: **Yisroel Itzikman** who died
In Rakishok 10th Iyar, 13th May 1927

For our Mother: **Chiyeneh Itzikman**
and sister: **Liebeh Shulman** and husband **Yisroel**
and their two children, who were killed by a
bomb dropped from a German plane,
as they were escaping from Kovno.

For our sister: **Bassel Gamburg**, husband **Velveh**,
and children who perished during the slaughter in Rakishok

For our sister: **Chaya-Devorah**, who died
suddenly in Worcester, America on the
5th Candle, Channukah, year 1928

For our uncle: **Yerachmiel Itzikman** and family

And for our aunt: **Mineh Wineberg**
Who were massacred by the hand of the
German executioners

We will be reminded and remember you

[from]

Rivka and Nochum Blacher and Sons
Yisroel and Abbo (Solly and Abe)

Reichel and Avrohom Gordon and children

In Memoriam
For our parents:

Father: **Shmerel**
[died in Abell, Lithuania, 1924]

Mother: **Soreh**
Murdered by the Germans

Our brother:
Avrohom-Moshe

Our Sisters:
Dobbeh, Riveh, Mineh

Who perished tragically during The national catastrophe
May Hashem avenge their blood!

[from] Yosef Shneider and family

We, the parents, stand with bowed heads
In memory of our precious son

Shnaier-Zalman Zakstein A"H

Who perished 16th October in an aeroplane catastrophe [air-disaster] during the Second World War, accompanying the American Military to the German front.
He is buried in Takeradi East Africa

In order to perpetuate his name, we have built a Hall in the Shul in Parys

With choking tears and yearning heart,
We will never forget you

[from] Harry and Fradel Zakstein
Parys, South Africa

For our Father

Mendel Leib Griz

who died in Johannesburg 1930

For our Mother:

Ella Griz

who perished in September 1941
in the Kovner Ghetto

[from]

Yitzchk and Winfred Griz and sons, Mendel-Leib and Zossel

....

May these lines stand
In eternal memory
Of our parents, Zaide and Bobba

Faivush Segal

died 23rd Tamuz 1941

Of our Mother:

Tziviah Segal

who died
In Kovno 29th Tishrei 1932

[from]
Hirshe-Michoel and Tzivia Segal
Chaya-Liebeh and Berel Ruch
and children

We mourn our parents,
Zaida and Bobba

Zalkeh and Soreh-Buneh Shapiro

Who perished in the
Poneveszher Holocaust

[from]
Daughter: 'Tzvia and
Hirshe-Michael Segal
Chaya-Liebeh and Berel Ruch
and children

....

We will always remember
our parents
Zaida and Bobba

Michoel and Tzeppeh Klug

Sister and aunt: **Liebeh**,

Husband **Chayim** and children

Brothers and Uncles:
Nechemiah and Moshe Klug

Who perished in Rakishok

[from]

Chayah-Ettel and husband Tzemach
Salomon – Pretoria

Leah Klug and family – Kovno
Feigeleh Lapp

Liebe Blumah and Aharon Ginzburg

For our Father: **Aharon Ginzburg** [Ortzik-Pesach's] – 2nd name not clear] who died In Rakishok 28th Iyar 1941

For our Mother: **Liebeh-Blumah** who died in Rakishok 19th Kislev 1929

For our brother: **Yosef Rafael**, wife **Rochel** and children who perished in the Rakishok Holocaust

For our sister: **Chana** and her husband **Herman Wagenheim** and four children

Who were murdered by the Germans in Dublin-Letland

For our sister **Feigeh** and her husband who perished in Vilkomir

And for all our relatives who perished

For our Brother:
Chayim Dov-Behr Ginzburg
who died in Parys, South Africa
7th Iyar – 13th May 1945

And for our Brother
Moshe Ginzburg
who died 20th Teivet Tashyäg,
2nd December 1952

May these lines [words] serve as a Memorial

[from] Yisroel and Yenteh Ginsburg
and family
Shmuel and Merel Ginsburg and family

Chayim Dov-Behr Ginzburg

For our Parents

Shlomo
and
Tzippeh Friedman

Who perished in Abell

May this serve as an eternal
[everlasting] remembrance

[from]

Abba Friedman and his wife

Johannesburg

Not one of you has a tombstone, so I, who remained living erect
a memorial, which will remember my father:
Baruch B"R Aharon Bakalczuk,
who perished in the destruction of Sernik, a shettetl near
Pinsk, in the month of Av, 1941

Rabbi Tzvi-Hirsh Bakalczuk

Rabbi Tzvi-Hirsh who was the Rosh Bet-Din
in Stolavitch and Deretshin White Russia.
My Brother **Rabbi [HaGaon] the genius Tzvi Hirsh Bakalczuk**,
who perished together with his wife **Chaya-Miriam**
in Treblinka and his children **Malka, Simeh** and **Moshe-Aharon**
who were shot to death in the Holocaust in Deretshin,
My Brother: **Yehuda-Leib Bakalczuk**, his wife **Chaya**
and their children **Berel** and **Aharon, Feigeh Malka** and **Brocheh,
Sheineh-Yentel** and **Rochaleh** who perished in the Serniker massacre
My Sister: **Esther-Goldeh Lande** who perished in the massacre
in Vohlin and her husband **Abraham** who died in Dambrowitz in the 1930s
My sister **Riveleh** and her husband **Hershel Fishman** and their children: **Aharon-Yitzchak,
Motteh** and **Zeldeleh** who perished in the
graves [pits] Morotshner Ghetto

[from]
Your son, brother and uncle
Melech Bakalczuk

May this be a hallowed memory

For our Parents

Chayim-Yerachmiel and Chaya-Batya Ruch

For our Sisters

Heinieh, Iteh, Keileh, Liebeh, Gitteh-Zeldeh and our Brother **Hirsh**

Who all perished in the Rakishok Holocaust

For our Sister: **Leah**

Who perished in Vilna where she was studying

For our Aunt and Uncle

Rochel and Zelig Zageh

who perished in Rakishok

For my Zaida **Elieh Hirsheh**

And Bobba **Zeldeh Reef**

who died in Rakishok

And for my whole extended family who perished by hand of the Hitler murderers

[from]

Daughter and son-in-law:

Ella and Leibe Osband and children
Reizeh and Asher Manne

We will never forget you

Our Father and Father-in-law

Itzik Baradavka

who died in Rakishok 21st February 1940

Our Mother and Mother-in-law

Ethel Baradavka

Our Brother and Nephew

Zalman Baradavka

Who perished in the Rakishker Holocaust

Our Sister and Niece

Eidel and her child

Who perished in the Kovno Ghetto

Our Sister and Aunt

Reizeh-Dobra Penkin [neé Ruch]

who died 28th February 1932

Our Brother-in-law

Katriel Penkin

Who died 24th June 1926 in Cape Town

[from]

Koppel Barkai [Baradavka] wife and child in Israel
Leibeh Davkin [Baradavka] wife and child
Asna and Abraham Furman, children
and grandchildren

May this be a memorial

Seated: Father: Hertzeh, Mother: Toibe-Riveh, Brother: Avrohom-Leib
Standing: Chaya-Dvorah, Soreh and Chasia

For our unforgettable parents:
Hertzeh Wingrin who died in Rakishok 7th Elul 1936
Toibeh-Riveh Wingrin who perished in the Kovno Ghetto

For our unforgettable Brothers and Sisters
Avrohom-Leib Wingrin and Wife **Henieh** who perished in Rakishok

Chasia and husband **Naphtali Wolk** and son who perished in Rakishok

Chaya-Dvorah and husband **Shaul Lubowitz** and four children
who perished in the massacre in D'vinsk

Soreh Wingrin who perished running away from
the Germans, from the Kovno Ghetto

We will remember you forever!

[from] Asnah Chait, husband and children – Pretoria
Malkah Levy and children – Johannesburg
Yisroel-Pesach Wingrin, wife and children – Johannesburg

As an elightened and eternal memory [memorial]

For our parents

Aharon-Natan and Irleh-Brochah Rubin

Who died in Philadelphia, North America

Tombstones: Irleh-Brochah [Front] Aharon-Natan [Back] Rubin

We and our families will always remember

and perpetuate your names in holiness

[from]

Shlomo Rubin – Johannesburg, South Africa

Hertz Rubin – Philadelphia, USA

Gitteh Ferman – Philadelphia, USA

Abba Rubin – Dartmore, USA

May this be an eternal memorial
Of our Mother: **Soreh-Rivka Rubin**
Of our Brother: **Shlomo Rubin** and wife **Rochel** and
their children: **Dovid-Leizer** and **Leibeh**

[from]
Chaikel and Soreh-Liebe Rubin, children and grandchild

We mourn the Destruction of Rakishok and Environs
and the demise [deaths]

of six million Jews

by the German Executioners

[from]
Business: Bacher, Aron and Co

May this be an eternal flame

For my Father **Hirsh Baradavka** who died
when I was a child
For my Mother **Etta**
who perished 15th September 1941
and my Sister **Esther Baradavka-Shwartz**
and husband
Shlomo who perished in the
Kovno Ghetto 15th July 1944

[from] Liubah Baradavkah - Israel

A memorial

For our Father

Fishel Levin – Ha Levi

And for our Mother:

Sheineh-Rochel

Who died in Uzbrkistan, having been evacuated [there]
During the 2nd World War
We will remember you forever!

[from]

Chaya and Binyomin-Michal Hurwitz and children – South Africa
Ethel and husband Avrohom Nussbaum – Canada
Beileh and Mendel Lerman – Canada
Soreh and Yitzchak Shneidman and children – Canada
Meier-Natan Levin, wife and children – Canada
Chaim Shimon Levin, wife and children – Canada
Yosef and Feigeh Levin and children – Vilna

....

In memory of all those

Who lie in the dust [sleep]

The departed of our family
and
Landsleit

H Orelowitz
Parys, South Africa

For the enlightened [illuminated] and dear memory of our
Father, Husband and Zaida

Menachem-Mendel B"R Yisroel Yosselowitz

who surrendered his hallowed soul on the
Holy Shabbat, Friday night while performing the
Kiddush, 6th Candle Channukah 1948.

He observed Torah and Mizvot, he kept Torah laws
and was a lovable and friendly person. He took great
interest in everything and in the needs of the community
In his home Shtetl 'Abell' he was a Gabbai
[a Shul official] in the Chassidic Shul and also
here in Johannesburg he was a committee member
of the Chassidic Minyan [Congregation]
He was also an important and capable worker
and member of the Rakishok Society

Mainly: The love of Israel [the Jewish People]
was very precious and holy to him.

In sorrow, those who remain

[His sorrowful widow]
His wife: Zeldeh Malka Yosselowitz
Daughter: Liebe. Son-in-law Moshe David Fisher
and children Soreh, Yonah and Pinchas Hertzl
Daughter: Elkeh. Son-in-law: Lipman Friedman
and children: Yehuda, Chaya-Musheh and Leah
Daughter: Rivka, son-in-law: Moshe Bunem Super
and children Natan, Ya'akov, Zorach, D'vorah and Rochel Leah
Daughter: Sarah, son-in-law Ya'akov Lifshitz and children
Daughter: Henkeh, son-in-law Avrohom Yitzchak Yachad
Ben Zion, Reuven and Leah
Son: Yisroel-Leib, daughter-in-law Esther
and children: Menachem-Mendel and Chayah Rochel

A Memorial

For my Father

And Mother

And the whole perished family

[from]

Yitzchak Shneider and wife

Randfontein, South Africa

For Wife and Mother

Chaya-Genendel Bat Shmuel-Micha Katz

Who died in Johannesburg

28th Nissan Tashyäb
26th April 1952

She was very charitable [righteous] with
Many beautiful qualities [attributes]

May her memory be hallowed!

[from]

Her husband

Daughters

Sons

Sons-in-law

Daughters-in-law

And Grandchildren

Herewith:
We erect an everlasting memorial
In memory

Of our dear Father

Yankel-Hirsheh Kur

Of our dear Mother

Soreh Kur

Of our beloved Brother

Faiveh-Behr

Who were massacred by the
cursed Nazi Fascist animals

We will always remember you!

[from]

Sho'al Kur
Braineh Kur-Rotholz
Yossel Kur
Leah Kur-Riback
-South Africa

Devorah Kur – Israel

Henech, Leib Mendel and
Michoel Kur and families – Vilna

In eternal memory of our parents

Standing: Moshe, Yisroel, Leah, Lana, and Chana-Rochel
Seated: Abba Yehoshua, Latteh-Gittel and No'ach

Abba Yehoshua and Latteh Gittel Visakolsky

Father died in Dusyat 3rd Tishrei 1931
And mother perished in Utian, witnessing the murdering
of her children who were shot before her eyes

Of our Brothers **Yisroel, Moshe and Noach**

Yisroel perished in the Rakishok massacre
Moshe fell in the [massacre] slaughter by the Germans in
the battles of the Red Army with the Germans
No'ach perished with his wife in Utian

We will never forget you and hold
your memory dear, forever!

[from] Leah and Nathan Brinkman and children – Johannesburg
Lana Visakolsky – Vilna

May this be in everlasting remembrance of our parents
Yitzchak and Chaya Davidowitz
We will remember you forever
[from] Abba-Leib and Sheineh Davidowitz and children
Malkah Witz and children

****

For our dear and unforgettable parents
Father: **Avrohom-Mendel Lubowitz**
Who died in Johannesburg 20th January 1939
Mother: **Ettel Lubowitz**
Who died in Johannesburg 16th August 1947
May this be a memorial
[from] Toibeh-Riveh and Leib Levitzky and daughter - Charkov
Soreh-Leah and Mottel Yaffe and daughters – Johannesburg
Chana-Mereh and Zelig Mendel Penn and children – Johannesburg
Shmerel and Yenteh Lubowitz and daughter - Durban
Chaim and Beileh Reizeh Lubowitz and children - Vereeniging

Menachem-Mendel Nachumowitz and Chaya Nachumowitz

May these lines be in everlasting memory

For our Husband and Father

Menachem-Mendel B"R Aharon Nachumowitz

Who died in Johannesburg
12th Teivet Tashyá
20th December 1950

For our aunt
Musieh Kalakur
with her children and grandchildren

For our uncle
Chayim Yitzchak Nachumowitz
and his family

For our aunt
Soreh-Dinah Shribnik
with her husband and daughter **Feige Rivkah**
All of whom perished in the
Rakishok massacre

[from]

Wife: Chaya Nachumowitz

Sons: Chloineh Nachumowitz, wife and child
Aharon Nachumowitz
Moshe Nachumowitz, wife and child
Avrohom-Yosef Nachumowitz, wife and child

Daughter: Gessiah-Rivka Jonas
Husband and daughter

May this be a memorial

For our Father

Moshe B"R Yitzchak Aires

Who died in Shvadoshtz

For our Mother

Pessia Aires

For our Sister

Soreh-Leah Pakawitz
with her husband **Leizer,** and their four children

For our Sisters

Taibeh and Yiskeh

For our Brother

Binyomin

Who all perished in Shvadoshtz

[from]

Chaikel Aires and children

Yitzchak and Sheineh Aires and children

We perpetuate hereby the name of our brother

Ya'akov Shmuskowitz

Hero of the Soviet Union and Finland

He was
Lieutenant General and chief of the
Soviet Airforce

He was the most capable in our family
His parents loved him dearly as their
first born and gifted [able] son

He completed a Russian 'middle school'
and for a certain time he studied at the
Yiddishe-Folkshul of the 'Kultur League'

He went to Soviet Russia and studied law.
He then entered the ranks of the Russian Army and
returned an invalid from the Japanese front
missing a leg [foot]

Never-the-less he still managed to establish
a great military career for himself
because of his great heroism and knowledge
of the art of flying, both as a pilot
and also as a theoretician, he became
Chief of the Soviet Air Force

In honour of his enlightened memory!

[from]

His Brothers

Aaron and Yerachmiel Moss [Shmuskowitz]
and their families

Durban, South Africa

In the holiest of holy memories

Of our Parents

Ya'akov and Guteh-Leah Kark

Of our sisters

D'vorah, Yochkeh and Yehuidit

And of our Brother

Leizer

Who all perished in Rakishok

And of our Brother

Leib

Who died in Rakishok in 1938

[from]

Yosef and Yehudit Kark and children
in South Africa

Yitzchak Kark, wife and child in Israel

Meier Kark, wife and children in Vilna

Ida Kark, husband and child in Vilna

For our Father

Dov-Behr Berelowitz

who died in Johannesburg 6th August 1935

For our Mother

Chasia Tzireh

who died 10th Sivan 1916 in Melitopol [Crimea]

For our Father

Shmuel-Natan Muskat

who died in Chaluwetz Province of Vilna 12th Sivan 1900

For our Mother

Feiga Bat R'Yerachmiel

who died 22nd Teivet 1925 in Dakshutz

For our Nephew
Chatzkel Berelowitz
who fell in the struggle for the Independence
of Israel against the Arab countries

He was the first of the South African
Jews who fell in the struggle for Israel

For the whole family Ruskind
Who perished in the great Holocaust

May these lines serve as an everlasting memorial for them all

[from]

Menachem Mendel and Chaya Riveh Muskat
children and grandchildren

For our Father and Brother

Meier Moss [Shmuskowitz]

Who died suddenly in Durban
5th September 1943

May this be an unforgettable memorial

[from]

Children: Zalman and Feigeh Moss

Brother: Aharon Moss, wife and children

And

Brother: Yerachmiel Moss, wife and children
Durban, South Africa

We present this Hazkarah [Memorial]

For our Father

Refael Gringut

Who died in Subat [Kurland] 8th Tamuz 1900

For our Mother

Esther Shlosberg-Gringut

For our Brother

Chayim-Yitzchak Gringut and wife **Matleh**
and their sons **Refael** and **Chone**

For our sister

Mineh and her husband **Henach Rozenberg**
and children

For our Sister

Soreh-Veleh and **Dovid Rosenberg** and children

For our Brothers

Arkeh, Shimkeh, Motkeh Shlosberg

and
For all our relatives who so gruesomely
perished in the Destruction Of Subat

[from]

Hirsheh-Leib and Rochel Green [Gringut]
With their children Eleh and Refael

An eternal memory for our
dear innocent parents

Yosel Raphael and Rochel-Rivka Ginsburg

Who were killed by the murderers of our
people with all the Jews of Rakishok

For our Sister
Soreh-Pessah Bunimowitz
and for our Sister
Chana-Musiah Ginsburg
who expired in the concentration camps
of the Nazis [may their name be obliterated!]

Their memory is engraved in us forever!

May their memory be blessed!

[from]
Yitzchak Ginsburg and family – Johannesburg
Tzipporah Ginsburg and family [Kimchi] – Chaderah
Hindah Ginsburg and family [Kutz] - Ramat Hashofeit
Pesach Ginsburg and family [Petersen] - America
Aharon Ginsburg and family – Vilna Russia

In Hebrew not Yiddish

The illuminated memory of my parents
who are interred [who sleep] in the dust of Rakishok
Father
Moshe Beynart who died in 1938
Mother
Chayah Beynart who died in 1933
Brother
Ya'akov Zelig who was killed in
Johannesburg by murderers who entered
his clothing business [shop]

[from] Zorach Beynart and family

In holy memory
Of my Father

Mendel Kuperman

Who died five days after Pesach 1940 in
Johannesburg
[from]
David [Dave] Kuperman and family

We stand in sorrow at the graves

Of our brother **David** and his wife
Of our Sisters
Reizeh, Leah and Beileh
Who perished by hand of
the Hitler murderers

[from] Yossel and Elkeh Perkis

We will always remember the names of our Parents:
Reb Yosef-Yitzchak Klein [Rosh Yeshivah]
of Rakishok who died in Poneveszh 8th Sivan 1927

and our Mother: **Mereh-Feigeh** who died on the road
during the evacuation of Lithuania in the First World War

Our Brother: **Menachem-Mendel** who died in Mexico

Our Sister: **Soreh-Leah** and her husband **Eliyahu Shneider**
and their child **Michoel** who perished in Kurshan during the
Lithuanian Holocaust

[from]
Shlomit and Yona Nanas and children [Israel]
Shoshana and Yechiel Leib Mindel and
children [South Africa]
Chana and Menachem Mendel Gandelman
and their children [Israel]

We express our deep and great sorrow over the
death of our Father

Michoel-Ze'ev
Who perished by the hand of the Nazi
animal in the year 1941

Over the death of our brother **Moshe**
and over the death of Moshe's one and
only little daughter **Frumkeleh**

who perished by the hand of the
German cannibals [may their name be
obliterated] in the year 1941

We will always remember you!

[from] Yitzchak and Yisroel Mikel [Michalewitz] - Johannesburg
Shimon-Yosel Mikel-Michalewitz – Pretoria
With their wives and children

For our Father
Hirsheh-Yankel Wiener
Who died in Abell –
28th Teivet 1914

For our Mother **Dobra Weiner**
Who perished in the Rakishok Holocaust

For our Sister
Malkah Zamelan [Weiner]
Who perished in the Rakishok Holocaust

For our Brother **Yudel Weiner**
who fell in the massacre on the Japanese Front 13th September 1945

For our brother-in-law **Leibel Zamelan**
who fell as a partisan in the struggle against the Germans

May this be an illuminated memory!

[from] Rivkah and Michael Feldman and Sons
Dinah and David Katz and children

May this be an unforgettable memorial
For our cousins
Yosef and **Batya-Ettel Shwartz**
and their son Yitzchak

And for all our relatives
and friends who perished
in Rakishok and Environs

[from] Feldman Brothers
and their families

For our parents
Mottel and Musheh-Batya Katz
For our Brother
Berel, wife and children
For our Brother **Yudel**
and sister **Soreh-Ettel Sohn**, husband and children
who perished in Sevenishok

May this be a memorial

[from] David and Dinah Katz
and children

Chayim Ya'akov Zakshtein

May this be a memorial for my husband

Hayim Ya'akov Zakstein
Who died in Johannesburg
15th December 1943

For my Father-in-law
Leibeh
and my Mother in Law
Henieh Zakshtein
Died in Abell

For the Parents
Nochum Nottel and **Pessel Pogrund**
Died in Abell

**Seated: Pessel Pogrund
Standing: Sister: Chieneh, Brother:
Reuven Meier Sister: Feigeh Bluma
Brother-in-law,**

For Sister
Feige Blumah,
husband and son

For Sister
Chieneh Pogrund

For Brother
Reuven Meier Pogrund

Who all perished in the
great Holocaust in Abell

[from]

Wife Tzippeh-Reizen Zakshtein

Daughter: Serah Yudelsohn,
husband and children.

Son: Nochum-Nottel Zakshtein

Standing: Brother Meier and [long may she live] Golda-Pogrund-Dick
Seated: Sister Tzileh, Mother Henieh, father: Yitzchak, Brother: Zalman

May this be a memorial stone for my Father
Yitzchak Pogrund, who died at the age of 77 years
He was a learned Jew, very religious and very loved in his home Shtetl, Abell and environs. He took part in the communal activity of the Shtetl and helped all the Shtetl institutions. He married off all his children. The youngest daughter married a young man from the Slabodker Yeshiva who lifted the spirit of the Jewish population in Abell.

For my Mother **Henieh** who died at the age of 77 years
She was the daughter of Eliyahu Zvi Peres
from Kupishok and was an educated and respected woman
For our Brothers: **Meier** and **Zalman** and Sister **Tzileh**

Apart from those from the Lithuanian Communities who were saved before the Holocaust, the children and the whole extended family perished with all the Jews of Lithuania

[from] Kalman and Nathan Pogrund and family – Cape Town
Goldeh and Chayim Dick and family – Johannesburg

Standing: Isser, Zalman and Leizer Koppelowitz
Seated: Mother: Liebe Koppelowitz

May this be a memorial for our Father
Nachman Koppelowitch
who died in Rakishok in 1928

For our Mother **Liebeh**
Who perished in the Rakishok Holocaust

For our Brother **Leizer Koppelowitch**
who perished in the Rakishker Holocaust

For our Brother **Isser** with his wife **Henieh [Yaffe]**
and their son, **Nochemkeh,**
who perished in the destruction of Rakishok

For our Brother **Zalman Koppelowitch**
who fell, 2nd November 1943, behind Oriel while fighting
in the ranks of the Lithuanian Brigade

[from] Nochum Leib and Rivka Koppelowitch and
children, Nachman Gittel and Pesach Koppelowitch

We will always remember
the tragic death
of

Berel Wingrin

and his wife

Rozeh

[from]

Elia and Henyeh Wingrin
Johannesburg, South Africa

....

May these few words
be a memorial for

Avrohom Dovid Chaitowitz

And his wife

Ettel

Their son **Rabbi Eliezer** and his son **Mottel** and
daughter
Hindeh and their families

Who perished in the last Great
Jewish World catastrophe

[from]

Maryasha Palavin

In Hallowed memory of
my father

Ya'akov Zak

May he rest in peace
Died in 1918

And my Mother,
Rivka Zak

May she rest in peace
Died in 1892 in Abell,
Lithuania

[from]
Binyomin Zak

....

In memory of my

Brother **Yitzchak** and his

wife **Sonia**
and their children,
**Mendel, Henieh-Rochel
and Zeldeh**

Who perished in Kavarsk in 1941

They will always remain in my memory

[from]

Shmuel Ichilchik [Hillel]

We perpetuate herewith
our unforgettable

Husband and Father

Chayim Moshe Gen

who died in Johannesburg
2nd Shevat 1943

[from]
Dina Genn and sons,
Yehoshua, Avrohom,
Yerachmiel, Gutman Sholem
and Zelig and families

....

For our Father

Dov Behr B"R Chayim Kremer
(nicknamed Berel Leah's)
who died in Rakishok
28th Iyar 1921

For our Mother

**Chayah-Soreh Kremer
Bat Reb Meier**

who died in Rakishok in 1941

May this be an
everlasting memory!

[from]

Shneier Zalman and
Liebeh Kramer and family

May the memory of our
Father be honoured

Yisroel Seratzhik

Died the morning after Shavuot
in Vilna in 1915

Of our Mother: **Sheineh-Dobra**
who died
10th Shevat 1948 in Malat

Of our Sister **Soreh-Leah** and her husband
Moshe Skurkewitch
and their children who
perished in Malat

Of our Sister: **Malkah Seratzhik** who perished
in Malat

We will never forget you!

Leibe and Esther Seratzhik, children and
grandchildren

....

May this be a memorial
For our Father

Shlomo Yehudah Fleishman
of Subat-Kurland who died in Darpat - 12th
Teivet 1910

For our Mother:
Frumeh Fleishman
of Subat-Kurland
who died 23rd Sivan Tarsà

[from]
Chana Leah and Hessel
Swartzberg and family

May this be an everlasting remembrance
for our beloved Husband and Father

Avrohom Yudel Kiel

Born in Varestzineh near Rakishok
Died 15th Cheshvan, 22nd October 1945
in Johannesburg

In sorrow [sorrowfully], those who
remained behind:

[from]

Riveh Kiel
Sheineh-Etteh, Yishayahu Levin and
their daughter – Johannesburg
Moshe-Behr and Gittel Kiel and daughter – Johannesburg
Ziseh and Meier Greenberg and daughter – France
Taibeh and Moshe Chayim Orlin and
children – Johannesburg

BELLA GOLUBCHIK

Bella was born in Johannesburg in 1938 to Ethel (Swartzberg) Aarons and Yerachmiel (Arsh) Aarons who were married in Lithuania in 1928 and emigrated to South Africa immediately after their wedding. They had four children Sam, (Sinisy). Alan (Hashalom), Bella and Judy. Both Ethel and Yerachmiel (Ralph) were ardent Zionists and loyal Jews, who were always involved in communal and charitable activities. Ralph's great interest and love was Hebrew Education. Among communal positions which he held over the years was Chairman of the Samuel Moch Talmud Torah (Mayfair Johannesburg), Chairman of the United Hebrew Schools of Johannesburg for many years and a place on the Executive of the Jewish Board of Education, also for many years.

Ethel was the 'Mrs Aarons' of 'Aarons Taiglach and Pletzlach' renown. Both parents were the proprietors of a manufacturing business, producing kosher sweets and nuts and of course Taiglach and Pletzlach. In later years they also imported goods from Franch (glacé cherries), dates from Iran and nuts from Spain.

Their home language was Yiddish which they spoke to one another, to landsleit, friends and family.

Yiddish was their language of communication with one another, with their landsleit, with most adult relatives and with many members of the community. To us, my siblings and myself, they spoke a mixture of Yiddish and English. In later years, mostly English. My Bobba and Zaida spoke only Yiddish to us, as they had no other language.

Yerachmiel was also proficient in Hebrew. Ethel was a fine linguist and spoke a number of languages. She was also a good mimic and had a mischievous sense of humour. They both acquired English (although Ralph never lost his 'Yinglish' accent) and eventually used English as the language with their children.

I learned to read English when I was about four years old. When I was sent to Crown Mines School at age six, the teacher found me reading and threw me out of Grade one "You can't read" she said.

"I can" I said and began to read to her from my little book and then the teacher sent me into Grade 2. I think her name was Miss Petkund.

I learned Yiddish by 'inhaling' it, from hearing, speaking and absorbing it through my pores. Reading the language was another matter.

One day when I was about eight years old, we arrived at 'Cheder' (by then the class was quite proficient at reading Hebrew) and Mrs Chaya Joffe (that remarkable little lady, of huge teaching ability) said; 'Kinder, today you will learn to read Yiddish' she then proceeded to write an Aleph 'This is 'o' and an Ayin 'This is 'eh' etc and she gave each one of us sounds and sentences to read and practice.... And thereby hangs a tale.

I matriculated at Mayfair High School, where I was Head Prefect in Form 4 and Form 5. Concurrently with my general education, I attended the Mayfair 'Cheder', the Samuel Moch

Talmud Torah, from the age of six until my matric year. I wrote Hebrew as an extra mural subject together with all my school subjects and obtained a distinction for it.

I then attended the Rabbi Avida-Zlotnik Hebrew Teachers' Seminar in Yeoville, Johannesburn and qualified as a teacher after writing the exams set by the Jerusalem University. Then I spent a year in Jerusalem, at the Chaim Greenberg Institute, affiliated to the University of Jerusalem, and received the additional qualification from the University of Jerusalem."

I began teaching for the United Hebrew Schools in their early morning (before school) classes and Talmud Torah Schools in 1960. I taught Metric and Pre Matric at Parktown Boys High in the 1960s and Matric and other classes at the Bernard Patley Talmud Torah in Yeoville and Matric and other classes at the Sydenham Talmud Torah in Johannesburg for many years.

In 1974 the 'Bat Mitzvah' Program of the United Hebrew Schools was 'standardised' and I became the 'official' Bat Mitzvah teacher for all the schools, except one or two which retained their own teachers. The syllabus was very comprehensive and intensive and at the end of the academic year the girls wrote an exam. I then had the task of preparing programs for the Shul ceremonies and coaching and rehearsing the girls for these. I taught Bnot Mitzvah pupils in Edenvale, Cyrildene, Waverley, Sandton, Pine Street, 9th Street Orange Grove, Berea, Yeoville, Houghton Primary School and Northcliff. I was also deputy director of the United Hebrew Schools for a number of years.
Mendel Z"L and I married in 1961 and have six children. We lived in South Africa until 2011 when we emigrated and came to live in beautiful Perth, joining some of our children.

Sadly Mendel passed away in April 2013 after a painful illness. It is thanks to Mendel that the translations of the letters for *The Pinsker Orphans* book were completed quite expeditiously as he kept 'reminding' me to sit down to do them.

IN MEMORIAM

Mendel Golubchik. 10 January 1925 – 23 April 2013
Menachem Mendel Gedaliah B"R Yisroel

Mendel was the most loyal and concerned husband and father. His love of family surpassed all else. He had a remarkable intellect and an amazing memory. Whenever a question arise about any subject, the reaction was 'ask Dad' and invariably the answer was there. He was a well of information.

He was interested in many subjects – classical music (he even learned to play the violin in his childhood), history, geography, people and the world around him. He was reading voraciously even almost until the day he died.

In addition to all this, Mendel had an astounding memory for jokes and a very naughty sense of humour. He was also a man of great integrity and honesty. He is sadly missed and always remembered with love and respect.

BOOKS COMPILED BY DAVID SOLLY SANDLER

***100 Years of Arc Memories* published 2006**
The Arcadia Centenary book contains the memories of over 120 children of The South African Jewish Orphanage.

***More Arc Memories* published 2008**
A follow-up of the Centenary book with the memories of more than 100 children.

This book includes a section of 17 chapters on the Ochberg Orphans.

***The Ochberg Orphans and the Horrors From Whence They Came* published 2011**
The rescue in 1921 of 181 Ukrainian War and Pogrom Orphans by Isaac Ochberg, the representative of the South African Jewish Community, from the horrors of the Pale of Settlement.

Half these children were placed in the care of Arcadia (The South African Jewish Orphanage) and half in the care of Oranjia (The Cape Jewish Orphanage).

The book tells of these horrors and the help given by the Jewish Communities around the world and contains the life stories of 120 of the 181 Ochberg Orphans.

***The Pinsker Orphans* published 2013**
The Pinsker Orphans book - in part a follow up of *The Ochberg Orphans* book - tells of the life and times of the children from the three Pinsk Jewish Orphanages in the 1920s and like *The Ochberg Orphans* book is but a small part of a much larger and forgotten part of Jewish History, the horrors suffered by the Jews in The Pale of Settlement between the two world wars. These horrors have been overshadowed by the Holocaust. The book also tells of the help given by the Jewish communities around the world, including the JDC, to their brethren in need.

The book contains details of the 44 Pinsker Orphans who went to South Africa with the Ochberg Orphans and 53 Pinsker Orphans that were taken to London, courtesy of The Pinsker Orphan Relief Fund of London.

It also contains the English translations of over 100 letters written in 1921 in Hebrew and Yiddish (translated by Bella Golubchik), by the Pinsker Orphans who remained behind, to Alter Bobrow their teacher and rescuer who accompanied the Ochberg Orphans to South Africa.

***This Was a Man* Reprinted 2014**
This book is the life story of Isaac Ochberg as written by his daughter Bertha Epstein and first published in 1974.

Reprinted with the permission of the family of Isaac Ochberg z"l with an addendum added.

***Memories of Oranjia, The Cape Jewish Orphanage (1911-2011)* published 2014**
The book is a collections of the memories of many generations of children (over 120) who were in the care of THE CAPE JEWISH ORPHANAGE which was established in 1911 in Cape Town South Africa.

The institution later adopted the name Oranjia and today is known as Oranjia Jewish Child and Youth Centre and still takes care of Jewish children in need in Cape Town.

PG compilation still to come

- Our Litvak and South Africa Inheritance
This book will tell of life in, and the history of Lithuania and South Africa from 1850 to 1950.
- The Ochberg Orphans - Volume 2

Charities benefitting from book sales

All the proceeds of the sale of these compilations go to Arcadia and Oranjia the two Jewish Orphanages in South Africa still looking after Jewish Children in need and to the JDC (The American Jewish Joint Distribution Company)

Please contact me on **sedsand@iinet.net.au** to order your books locally and have them delivered to friends and family around the world

Best wishes good health and *Shalom*

David

David Solly Sandler
Perth Western Australia

www.ingramcontent.com/pod-product-compliance
Lightning Source LLC
Chambersburg PA
CBHW080749300426
44114CB00019B/2673